VOL. 15

HAL•LEONARD
BASS PLAY-ALONG

MAINSTREAM ROCK

ISBN 978-1-4234-1428-5

HAL•LEONARD®
CORPORATION
7777 W. BLUEMOUND RD. P.O. BOX 13819 MILWAUKEE, WI 53213

Visit Hal Leonard Online at
www.halleonard.com

Bass Notation Legend

Bass music can be notated two different ways: on a *musical staff*, and in *tablature*.

THE MUSICAL STAFF shows pitches and rhythms and is divided by bar lines into measures. Pitches are named after the first seven letters of the alphabet.

TABLATURE graphically represents the bass fingerboard. Each horizontal line represents a string, and each number represents a fret.

3rd string, open 2nd string, 2nd fret 1st & 2nd strings open, played together

HAMMER-ON: Strike the first (lower) note with one finger, then sound the higher note (on the same string) with another finger by fretting it without picking.

PULL-OFF: Place both fingers on the notes to be sounded. Strike the first note and without picking, pull the finger off to sound the second (lower) note.

LEGATO SLIDE: Strike the first note and then slide the same fret-hand finger up or down to the second note. The second note is not struck.

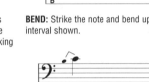

SHIFT SLIDE: Same as legato slide, except the second note is struck.

TRILL: Very rapidly alternate between the notes indicated by continuously hammering on and pulling off.

TREMOLO PICKING: The note is picked as rapidly and continuously as possible.

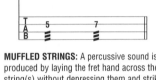

VIBRATO: The string is vibrated by rapidly bending and releasing the note with the fretting hand.

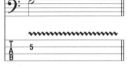

SHAKE: Using one finger, rapidly alternate between two notes on one string by sliding either a half-step above or below.

NATURAL HARMONIC: Strike the note while the fret hand lightly touches the string directly over the fret indicated.

Harm.

12

MUFFLED STRINGS: A percussive sound is produced by laying the fret hand across the string(s) without depressing them and striking them with the pick hand.

BEND: Strike the note and bend up the interval shown.

1/2

BEND AND RELEASE: Strike the note and bend up as indicated, then release back to the original note. Only the first note is struck.

1/2

RIGHT-HAND TAP: Hammer ("tap") the fret indicated with the "pick-hand" index or middle finger and pull off to the note fretted by the fret hand.

LEFT-HAND TAP: Hammer ("tap") the fret indicated with the "fret-hand" index or middle finger.

SLAP: Strike ("slap") string with right-hand thumb.

T

POP: Snap ("pop") string with right-hand index or middle finger.

P

Additional Musical Definitions

> (accent) · Accentuate note (play it louder).

^ (accent) · Accentuate note with great intensity.

. (staccato) · Play the note short.

⊓ · Downstroke

∨ · Upstroke

D.S. al Coda · Go back to the sign (%), then play until the measure marked "***To Coda***," then skip to the section labelled "**Coda**."

D.C. al Fine · Go back to the beginning of the song and play until the measure marked "***Fine***" (end).

Bass Fig. · Label used to recall a recurring pattern.

Fill · Label used to identify a brief melodic figure which is to be inserted into the arrangement.

tacet · Instrument is silent (drops out).

· Repeat measures between signs.

1. 2. · When a repeated section has different endings, play the first ending only the first time and the second ending only the second time.

NOTE: Tablature numbers in parentheses mean:
1. The note is being sustained over a system (note in standard notation is tied), or
2. The note is sustained, but a new articulation (such as a hammer-on, pull-off, slide or vibrato) begins, or
3. The note is a barely audible "ghost" note (note in standard notation is also in parentheses).

CONTENTS

Are You Gonna Be My Girl

Words and Music by Cameron Muncey and Nicholas Cester

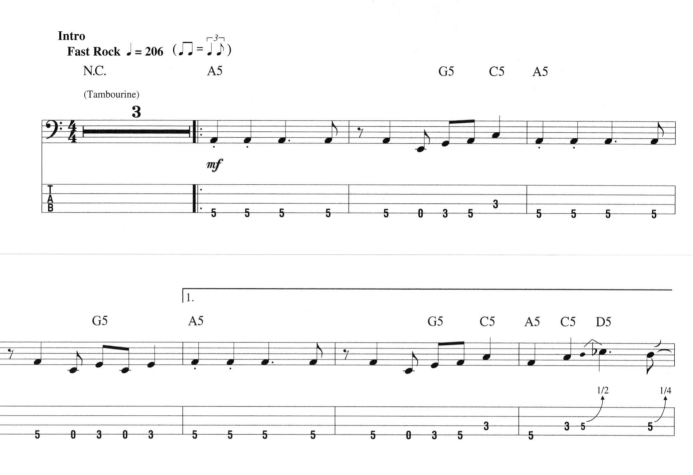

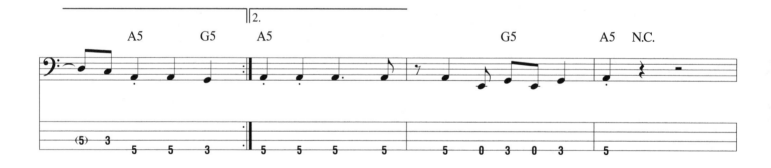

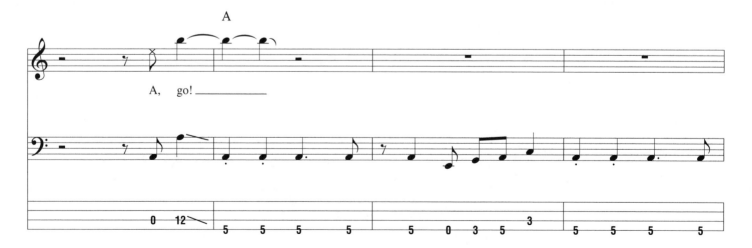

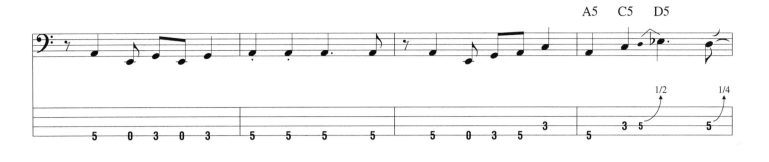

Verse

1. So, one, two, three, take my hand and come with me be-cause you

look so fine that I real-ly want to make you mine.

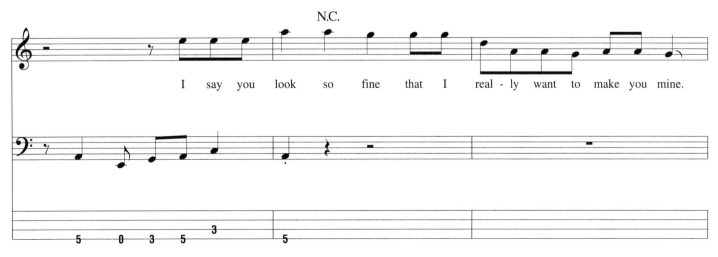

I say you look so fine that I real-ly want to make you mine.

Well, four, five, six, come on ____ ____ and get your kicks. Now you don't need mon-ey { when you look like that, do you, hon-ey? / with a face like that, do ya? ____ }

Pre-Chorus

Big ____ black boots, long ____ brown hair. ____

Chorus

be - fore I let _____ you get a - way, _____ yeah. __

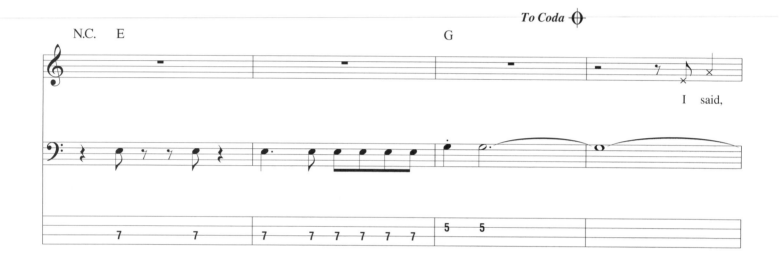

To Coda ⊕

N.C. E   G

I said,

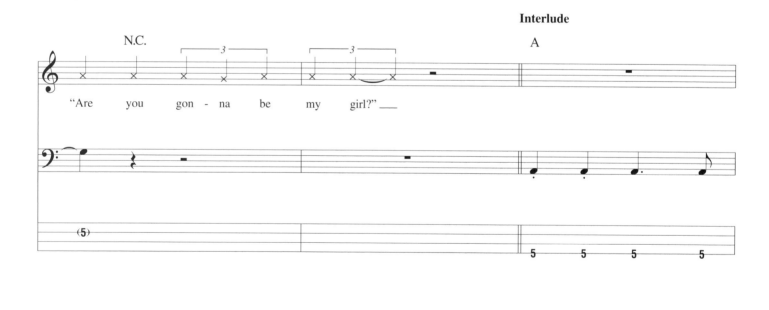

Interlude

N.C.

"Are you gon - na be my girl?" __

A

C5   D5   A5   G5

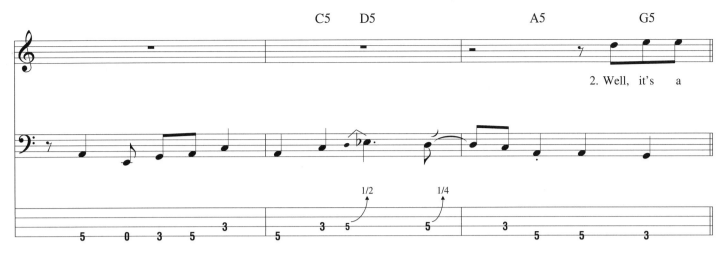

2. Well, it's a

Coda

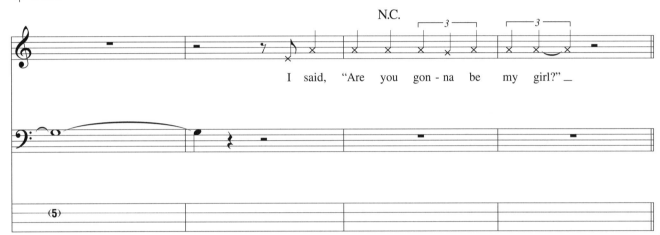

N.C.

I said, "Are you gon - na be my girl?" ___

Interlude

A

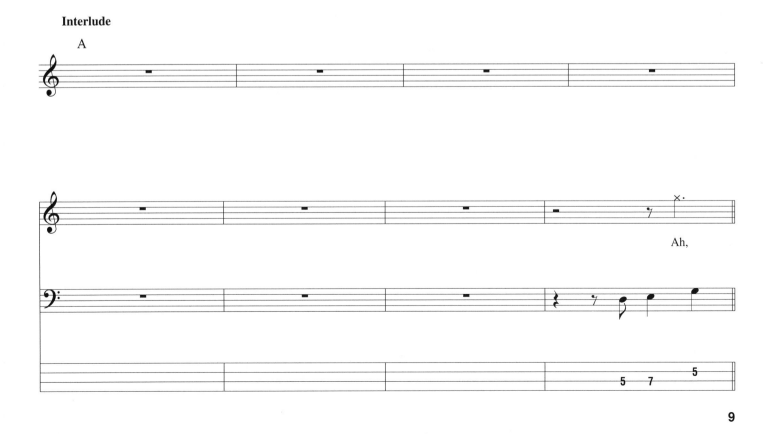

Ah,

Guitar Solo

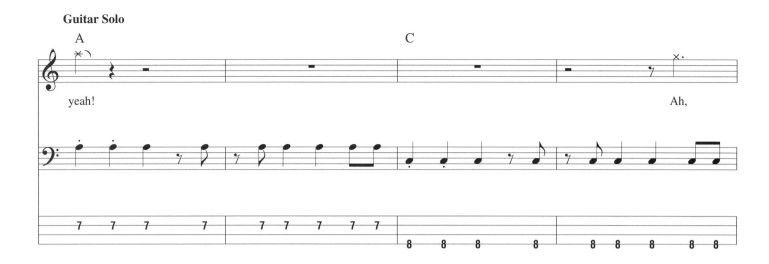

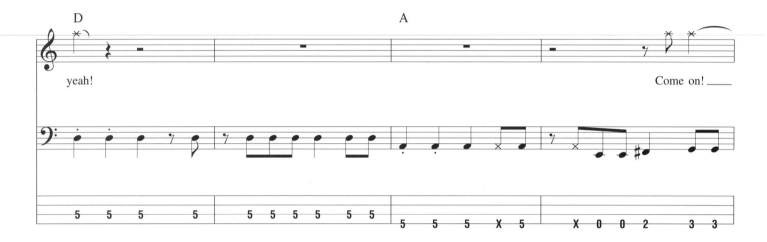

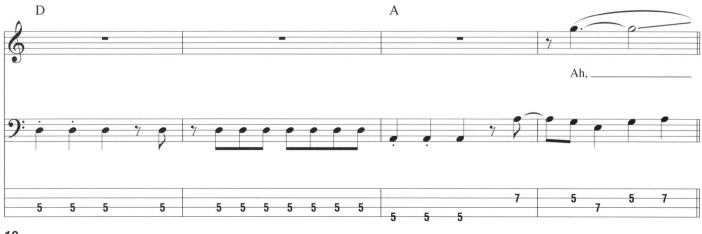

Chorus

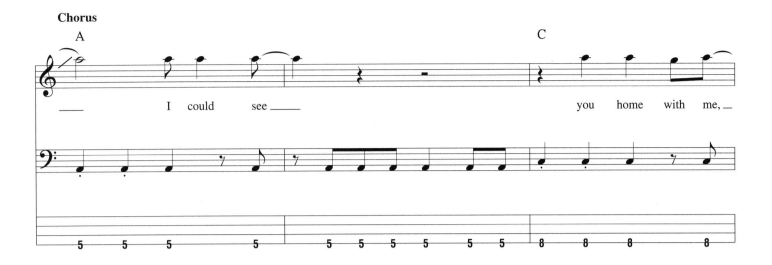

I could see you home with me,

but you were with an - oth - er man,

yeah. I know

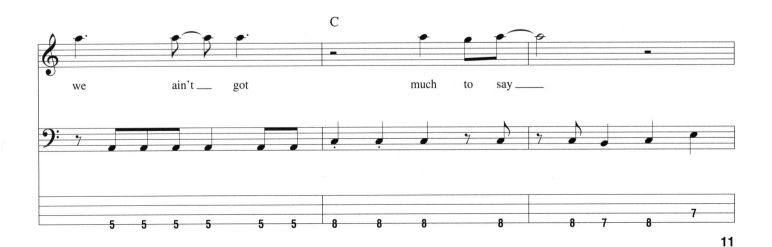

we ain't got much to say

be - fore I let you get a - way, yeah.

Outro

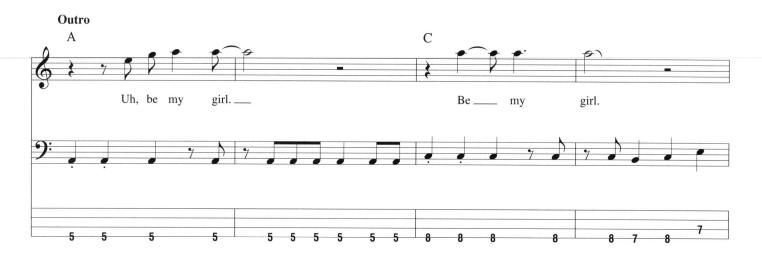

Uh, be my girl. Be my girl.

Are you gon - na be my girl?

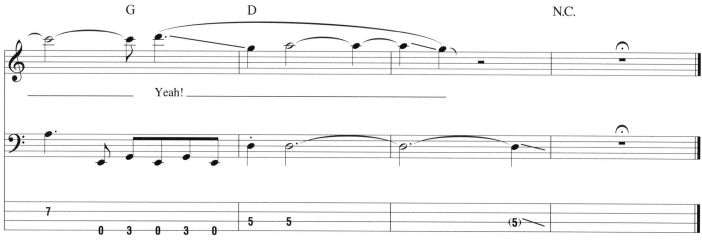

Yeah!

Be Yourself

Lyrics by Chris Cornell
Music written and arranged by Audioslave

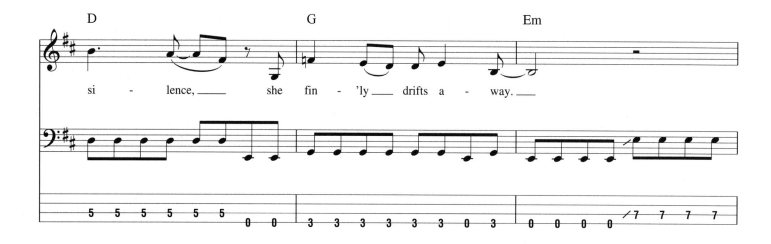

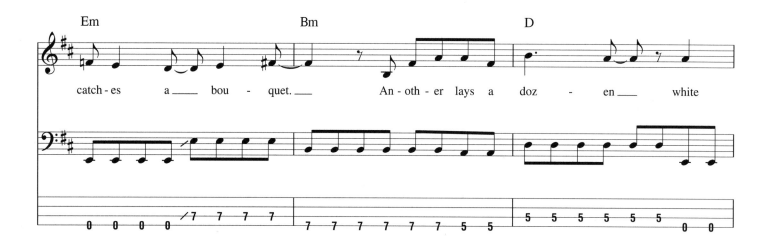

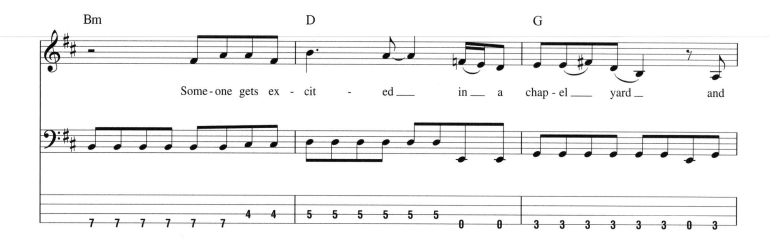

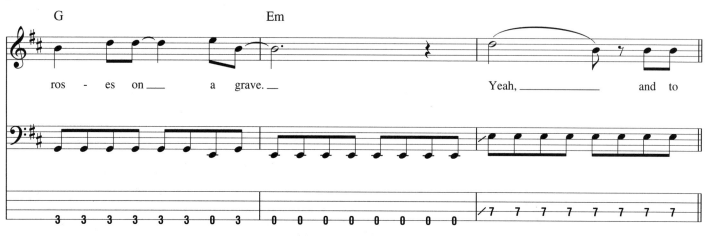

14

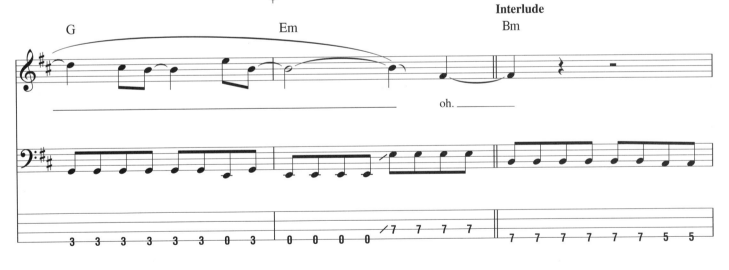

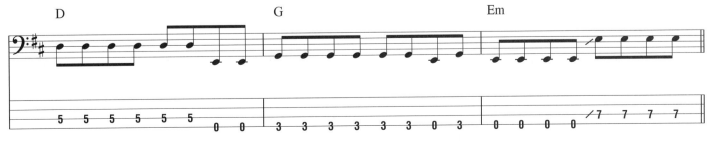

Sep-'rate or u - nit - ed, _____ health - y or ___ in -

D.S. al Coda ⊕ **Coda**

sane. _____ And to

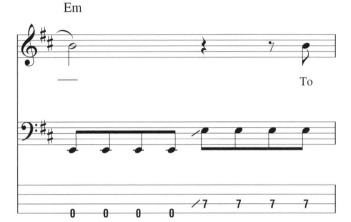

_ To

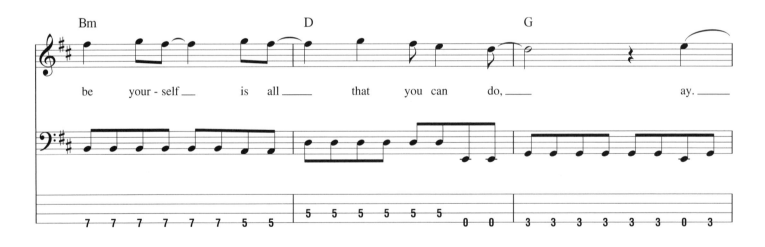

be your - self ___ is all ____ that you can do, ____ ay. ___

_____ Be your - self ___ is all _____ that you can do. _

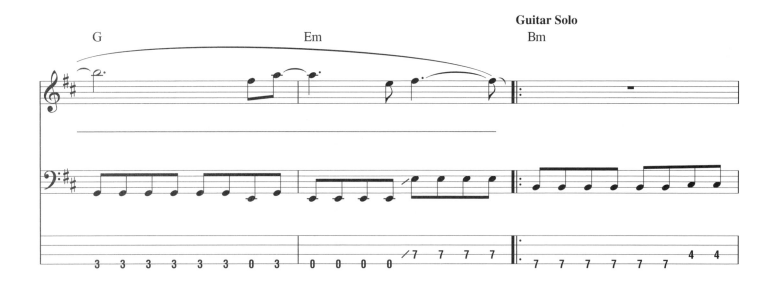

Guitar Solo

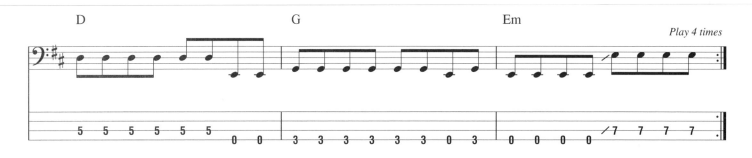

Play 4 times

Bridge

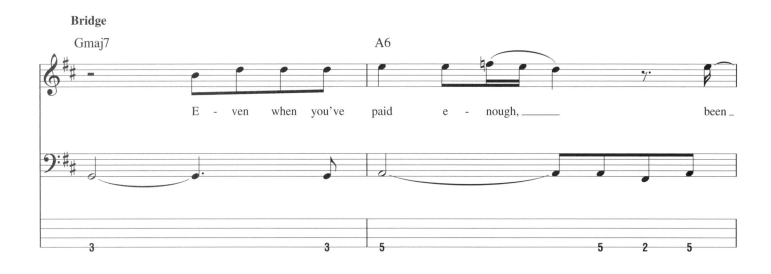

E - ven when you've paid e - nough,_____ been _____

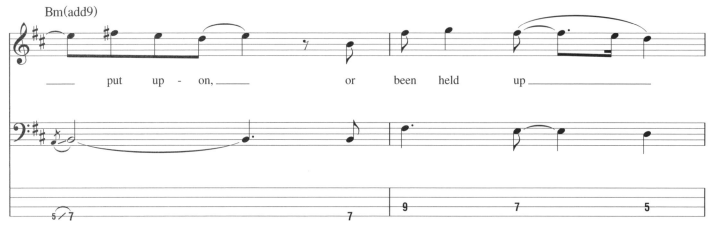

_____ put up - on,_____ or been held up _____

with ev - 'ry sin - gle mem - 'ry of _____ the good or bad, _____

fac - es _ of _ luck. _____ Don't lose an - y sleep to - night, _ I'm sure _

_ ev - 'ry - thing _ will end up _ al - right. _____ You may win or

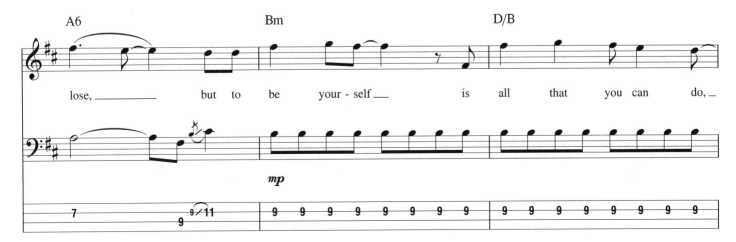

lose, _____ but to be your - self _ is all that you can do, _

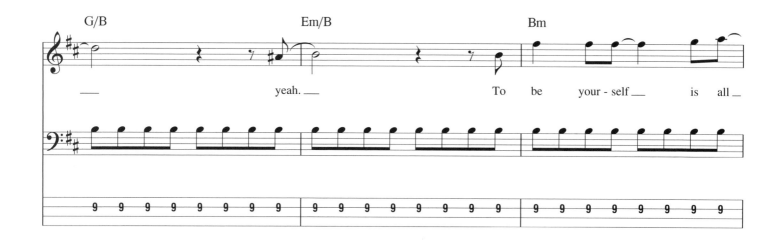

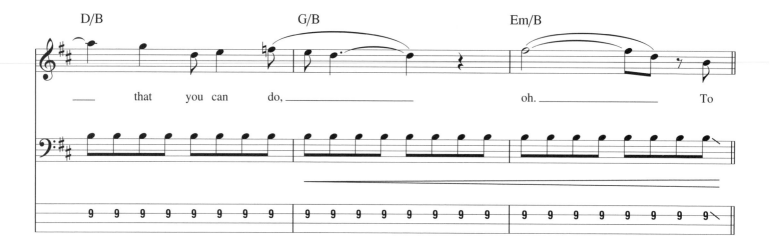

Chorus

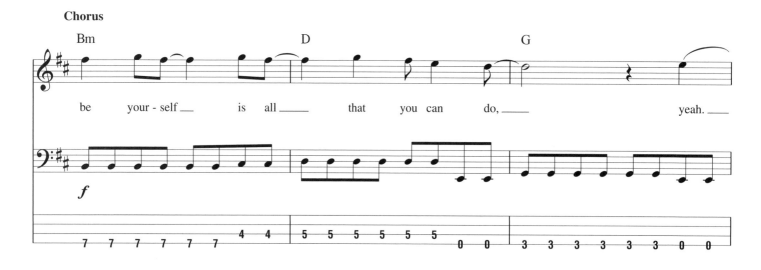

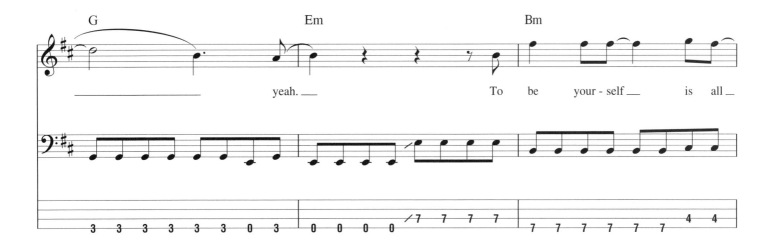

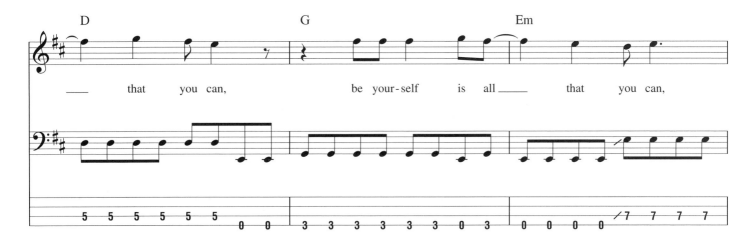

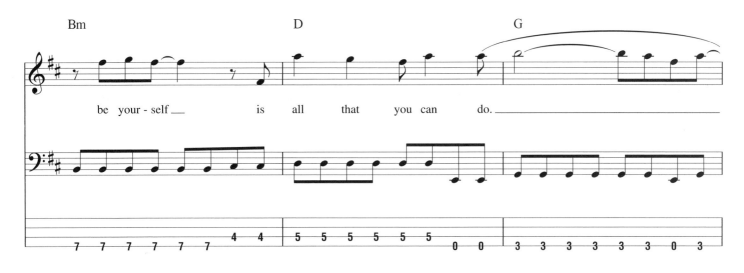

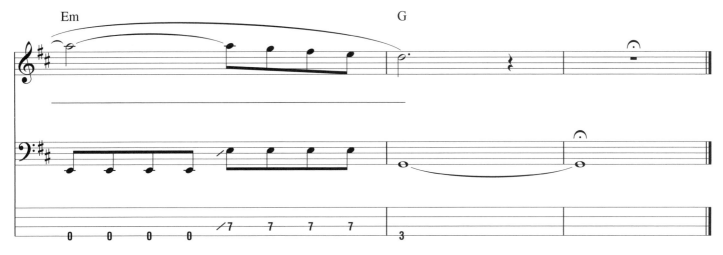

By the Way

Words and Music by Anthony Kiedis, Flea, John Frusciante and Chad Smith

Drop D tuning:
(low to high) D-A-D-G

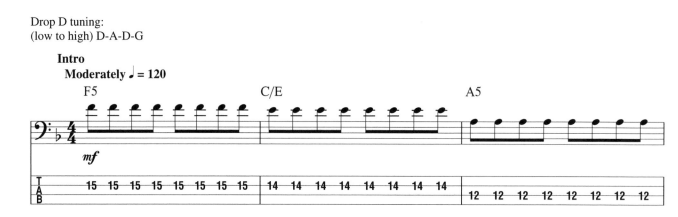

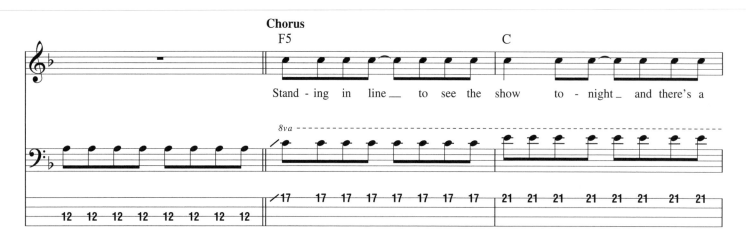

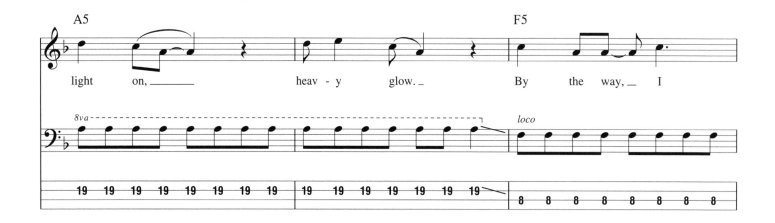

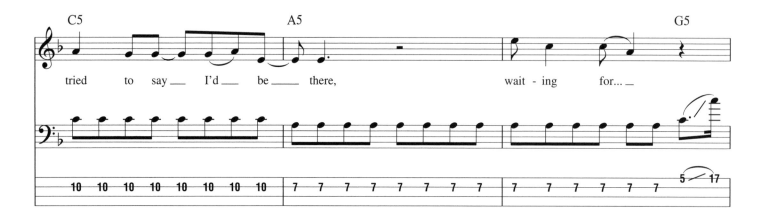

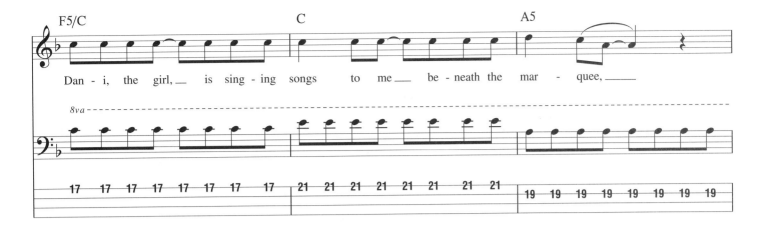

Dan - i, the girl,___ is sing - ing songs to me ___ be - neath the mar - quee,___

Interlude

o - ver - load. ___

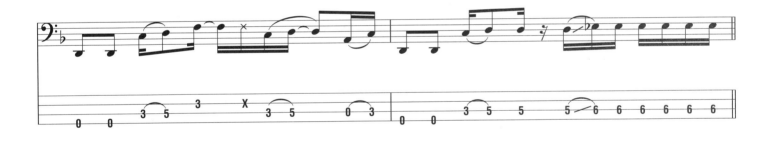

𝄋 **Verse**

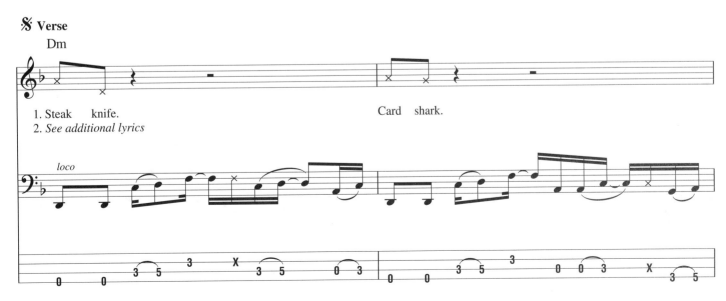

1. Steak knife.   Card shark.
2. *See additional lyrics*

Rib cage. Soft tail.

Chorus

F   C   Dm

Stand-ing in line ___ to see the show to-night ___ and there's a light on, ___

F   C

heav-y glow. ___ By the way, ___ I tried to say ___ I'd be ___

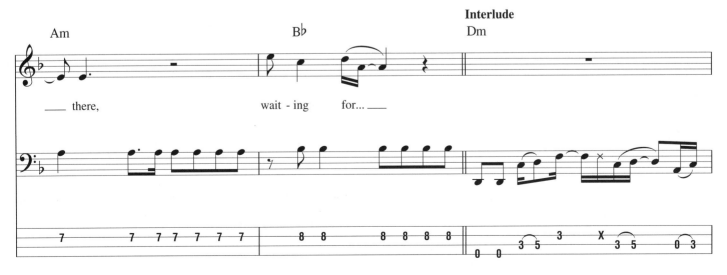

Am   B♭   **Interlude** Dm

___ there, wait-ing for... ___

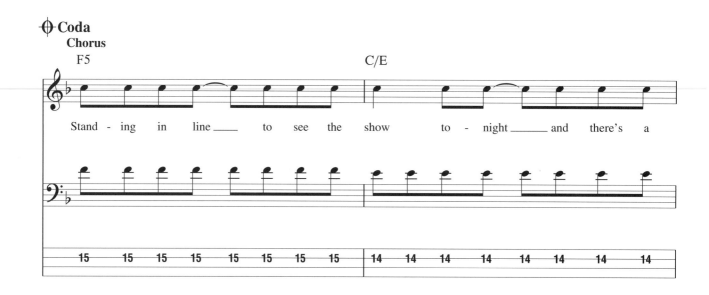

Coda

Chorus

Stand - ing in line ____ to see the show to - night _____ and there's a

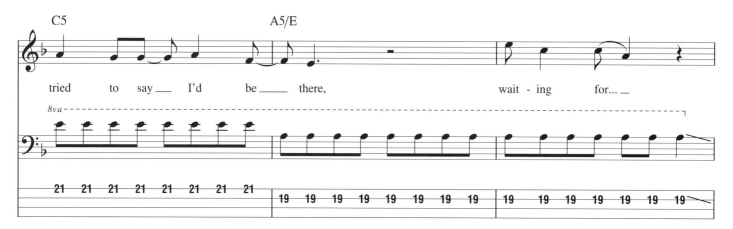

light on, _____ heav - y glow. __ By the way, __ I

tried to say ___ I'd be ___ there, wait - ing for... __

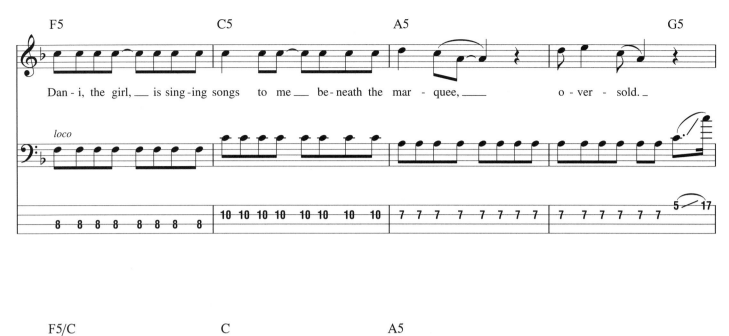

Dan - i, the girl, ___ is sing -ing songs to me ___ be - neath the mar - quee, ___ o - ver - sold. _

By the way, _ I tried to say _ I'd be ___ there, wait - ing for... _____

Interlude

Dm

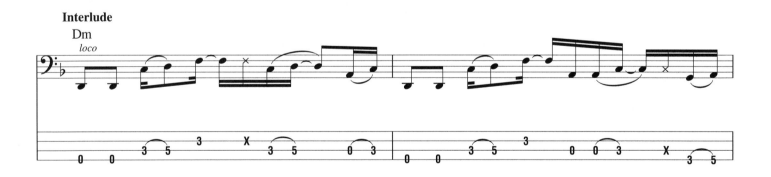

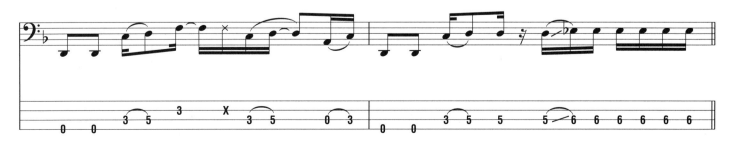

Bridge

Dm

Chorus

F   C   Dm

Stand-ing in line ___ to see the show to-night ___ and there's a light on, ___

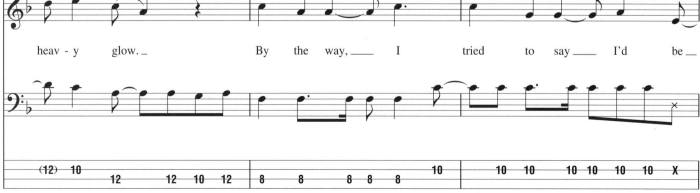

F   C

heav-y glow. ___ By the way, ___ I tried to say ___ I'd be ___

28

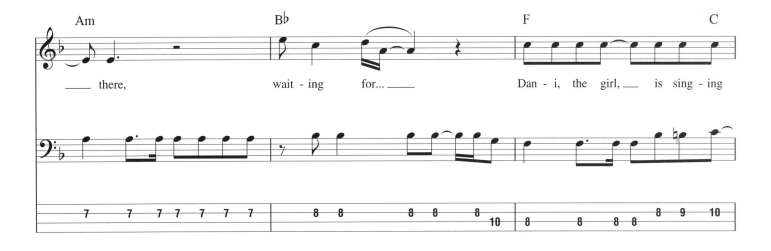

_____ there, wait - ing for... _____ Dan - i, the girl, _____ is sing - ing

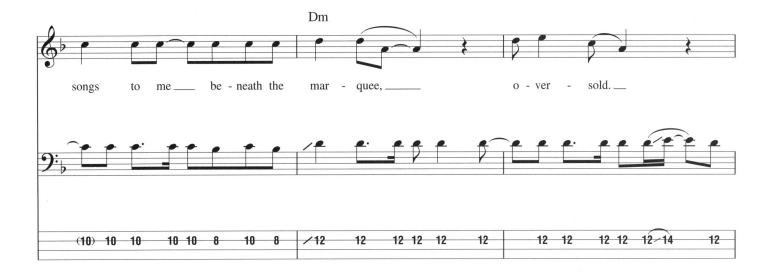

songs to me _____ be - neath the mar - quee, _____ o - ver - sold. _____

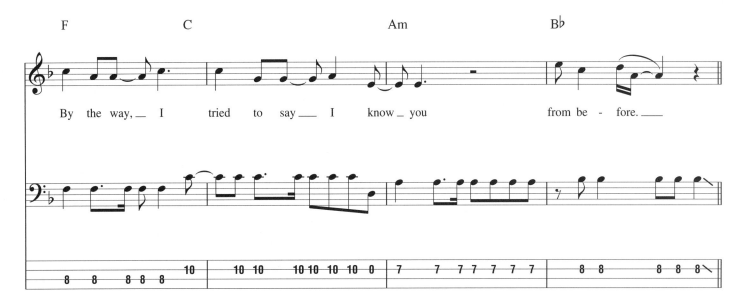

By the way, _ I tried to say _ I know _ you from be - fore. _____

Outro-Chorus

Additional Lyrics

2. *Spoken:* *Blackjack. Dope dick. Pawn shop. Quick pick.*
Kiss that dyke, I know you want to hold one.
Not on strike, but I'm about to bowl one.
Bite that mic, I know you never stole one.
Girls that like a story, so I told one.
Song bird. Main line. Cash back. Hard top.

Clocks

Words and Music by Guy Berryman, Jon Buckland, Will Champion and Chris Martin

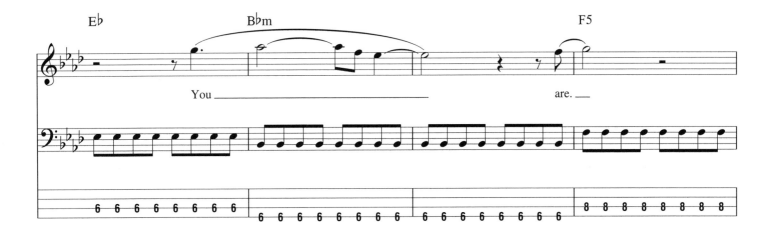

You ___

are. ___

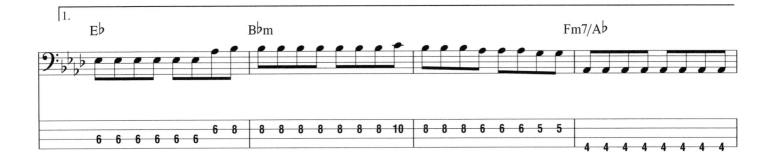

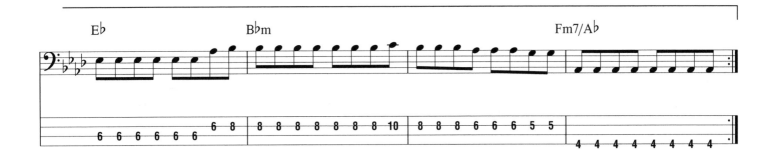

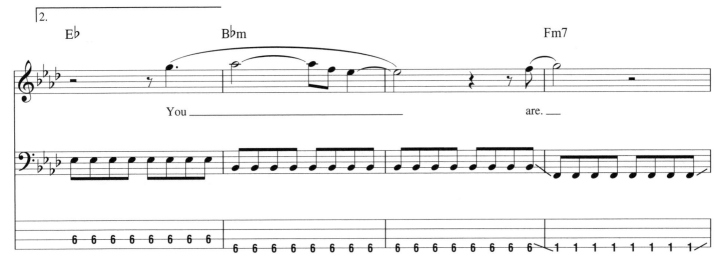

You ___

are. ___

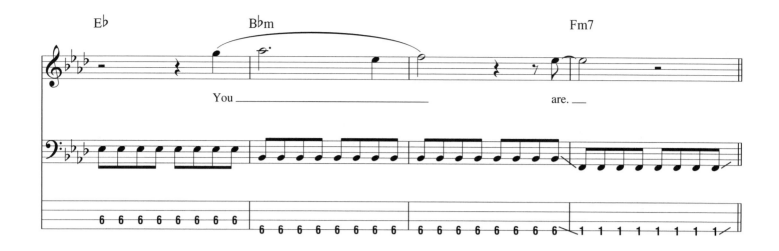

You _____ are. ___

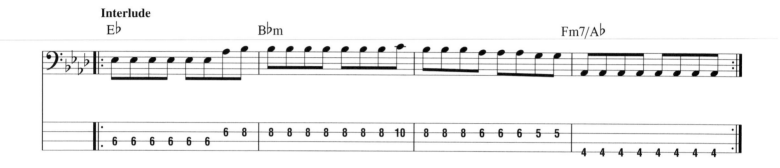

Interlude

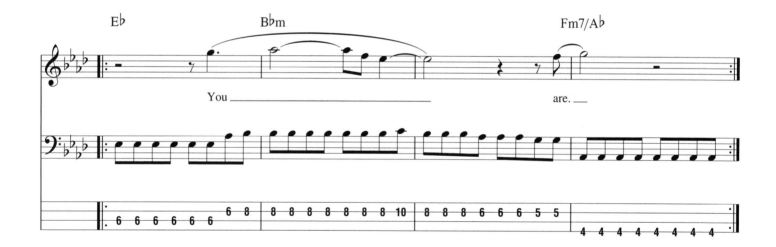

You _____ are. ___

Bridge

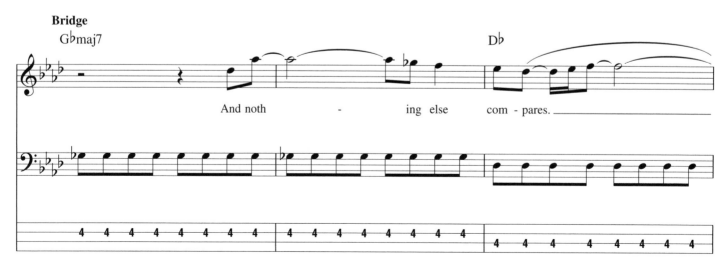

And noth - ing else com - pares. ___

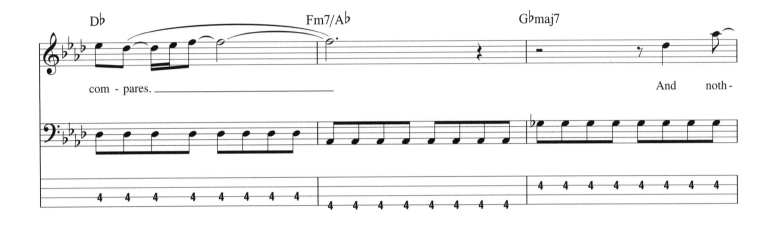

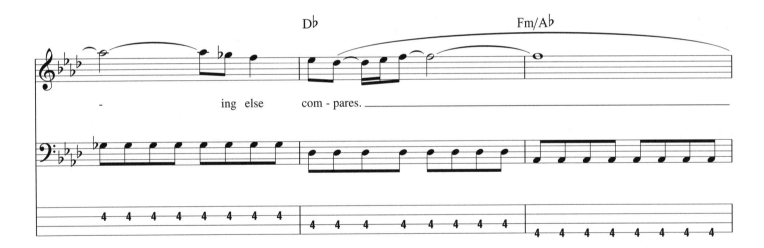

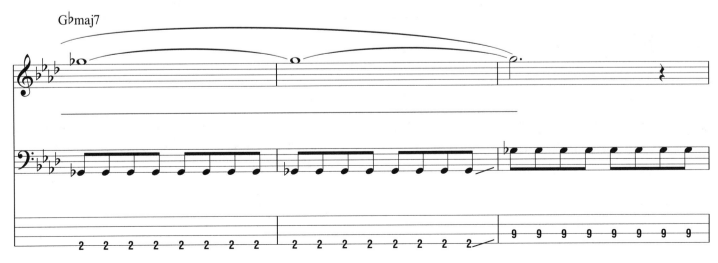

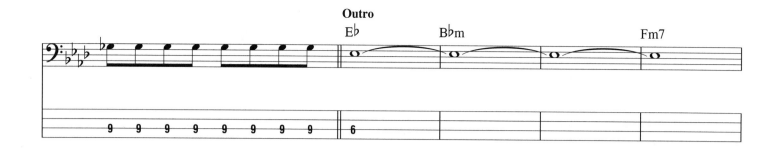

Outro

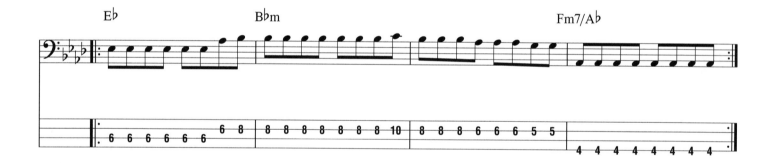

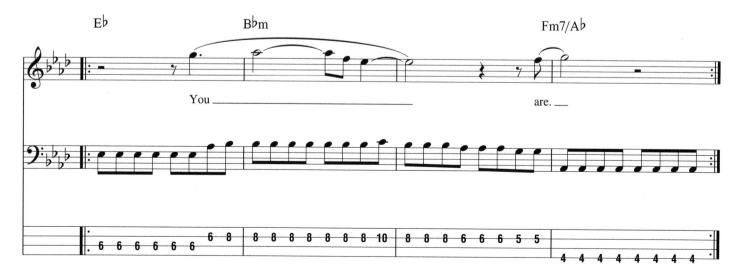

You _____ are. ____

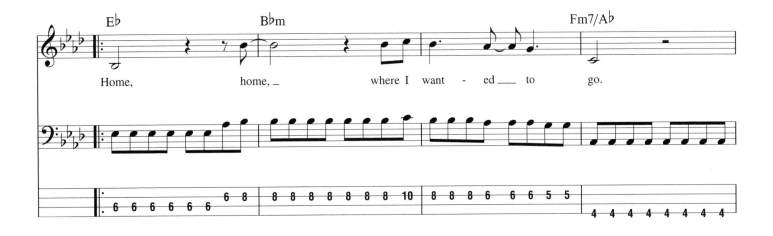

Home, home, _____ where I want - ed ___ to go.

Home, home, where I want - ed ___ to go.

Play 4 times & fade

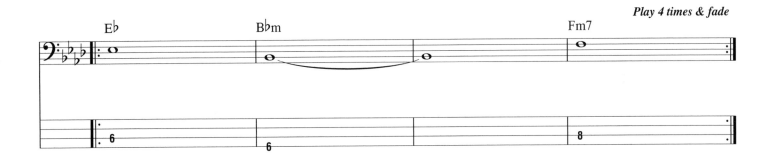

Additional Lyrics

2. Confusion that never stops, closing walls and tickin' clocks.
   Gonna come back and take you home, I could not stop, that you now know.
   Singin': come out upon my seas, cursed missed opportunities.
   Am I a part of the cure, or am I part of the disease?

Heaven

Words and Music by Henry Garza, Joey Garza and Ringo Garza

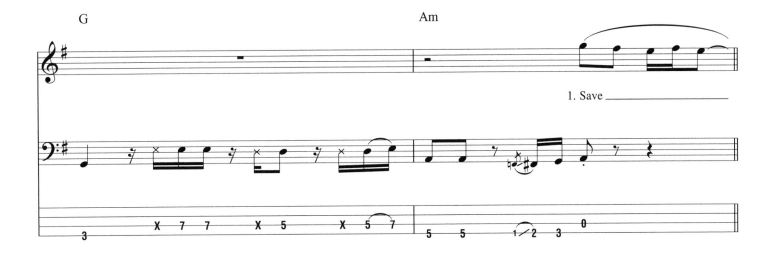

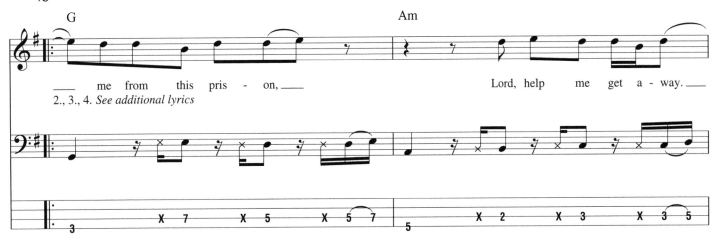

§ Verse

me from this pris - on, ___

Lord, help me get a - way.

2., 3., 4. *See additional lyrics*

3rd & 4th times, substitute Fill 1

'Cause on -

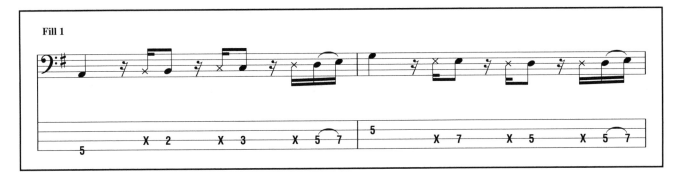

Fill 1

D.S. al Coda 1

⊕ Coda 1

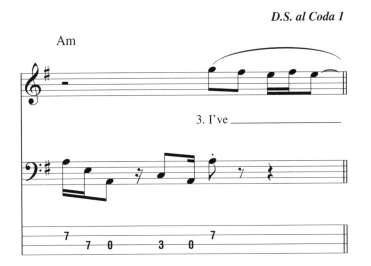

3. I've _____

Yeah, ___   Lord, can you tell   me?

'Cause I just   got   to   know _ how   far, _

___ yeah.

Yeah,   Lord,   can you tell   me?

Guitar Solo

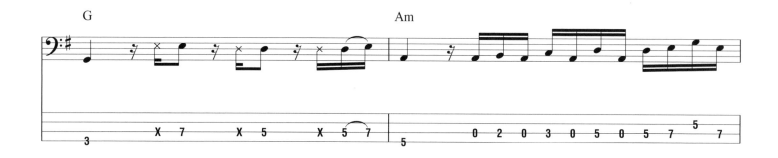

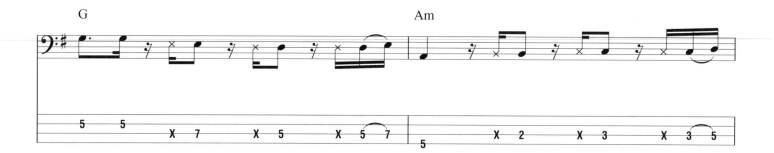

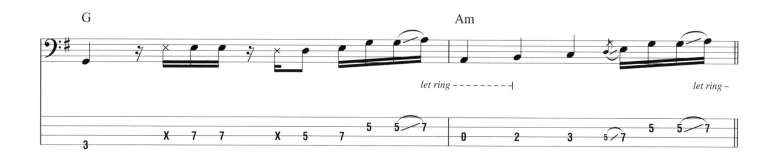

Bridge

Tú que es - tás___ en - trad - o al ci - el - o,___

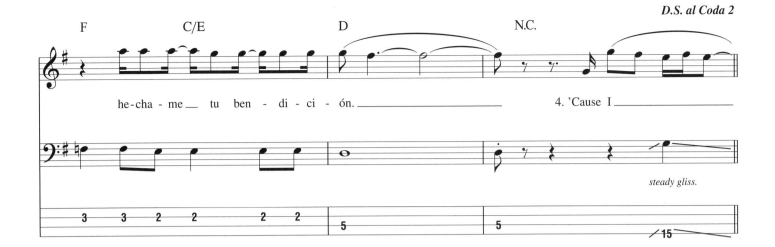

he-cha-me___ tu ben - di - ci - ón._____ 4. 'Cause I_____

steady gliss.

Coda 2

Yeah,   Lord, can you tell   me?

'Cause I just   got   to know___ how   far, ___   yeah.

Yeah,   Lord,   can you tell   me?

'Cause I just got - ta know how far. _____

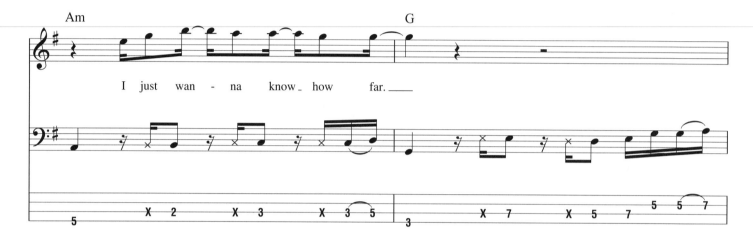

I just wan - na know how far. _____

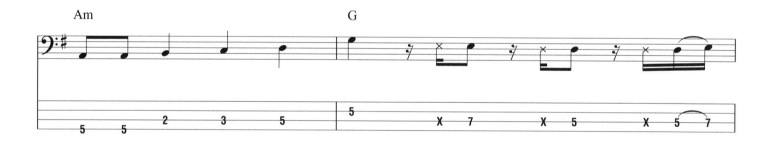

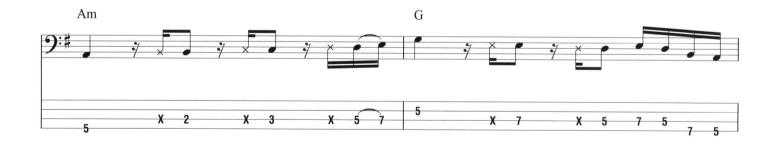

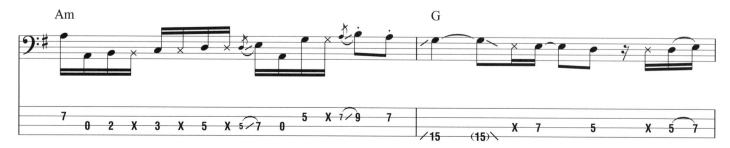

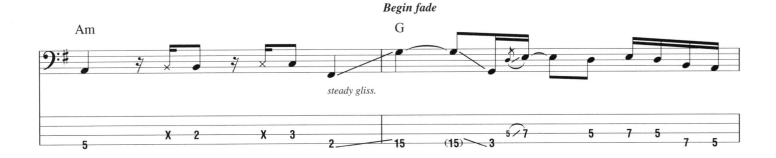

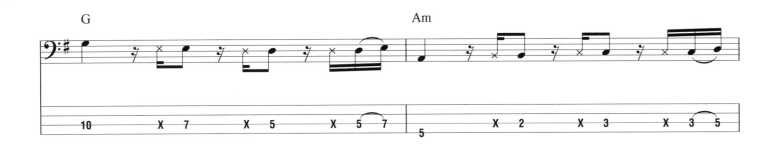

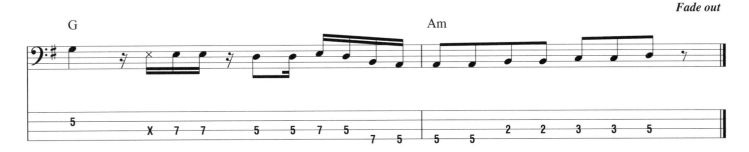

Additional Lyrics

2. I've been lost in my own place and I'm gettin' weary.
   (How far is heaven?)
   And I know that I need to change my ways of livin'.
   (How far is heaven?)
   Lord, can you tell me?

3. I've been locked up way too long in this crazy world.
   (How far is heaven?)
   And I'll just keep on prayin', Lord, and just keep on livin'.
   (How far is heaven?)
   Yeah, Lord, can you tell me?
   (How far is heaven?)
   'Cause I just got to know how far, yeah.
   (How far is heaven?)
   Yeah, Lord, can you tell me?

4. 'Cause I know there's a better place than this place I'm livin'.
   (How far is heaven?)
   And I just got to have some faith, and just keep on giving.
   (How far is heaven?)
   Yeah, Lord, can you tell me?
   (How far is heaven?)
   'Cause I just got to know how far, yeah.
   (How far is heaven?)
   Yeah, Lord, can you tell me?
   (How far is heaven?)
   'Cause I just gotta know how far.

I Did It

Words and Music by David J. Matthews and Glen Ballard

5-stg. bass:
(low to high) B-E-A-D-G

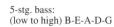

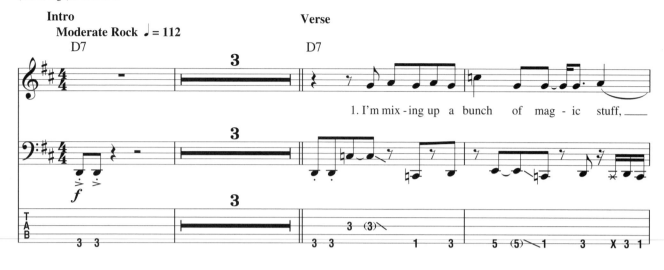

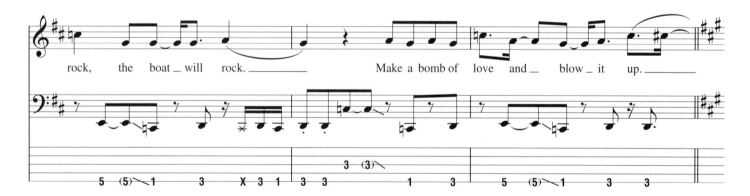

C#5

I o-pen up the cur-tains, I___ heard si - rens there,___ the lights flash and crawl.___

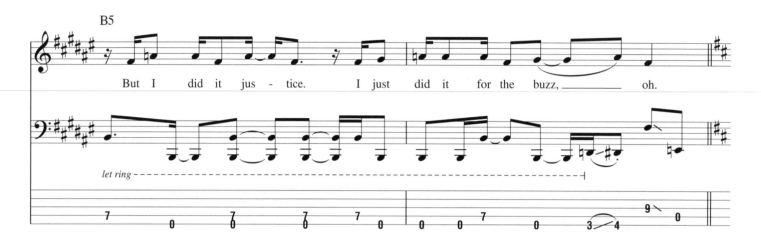

B5

But I did it jus - tice. I just did it for the buzz,_____ oh.

let ring -

Verse

D7

2. It's a nick-el or a dime for what_ I've done._____ The truth is that I

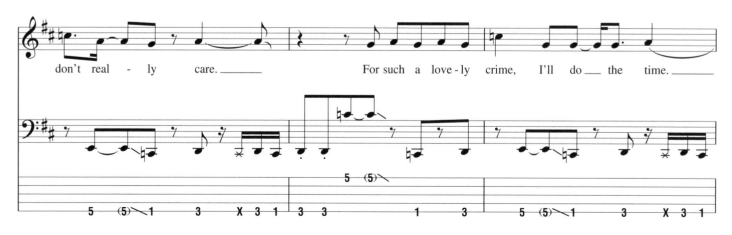

don't real - ly care.____ For such a love-ly crime, I'll do___ the time.____

Chorus

You bet-ter lock me up, I'll do it a-gain. I did it. Do you think I've gone too far? I did it. Guilt-y as charged. I did it. It was me, right or wrong. I did it.

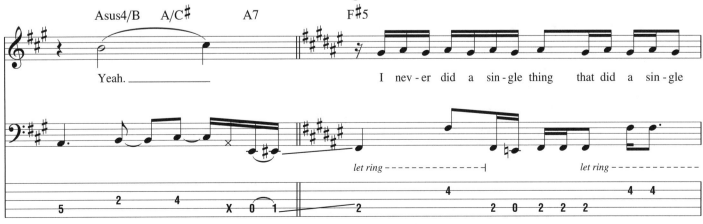

Bridge

Yeah. I nev-er did a sin-gle thing that did a sin-gle

thing to change _ the ug - ly ways of the world. I did-n't know it felt _ so right _ in - side, _

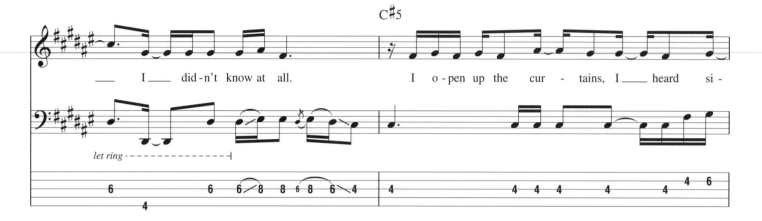

_ I _ did-n't know at all. I o-pen up the cur - tains, I _ heard si -

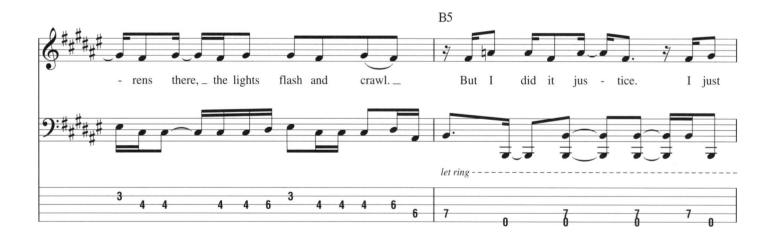

- rens there, _ the lights flash and crawl. _ But I did it jus - tice. I just

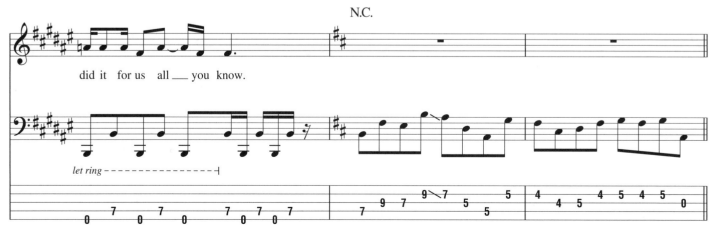

did it for us all _ you know.

Chorus

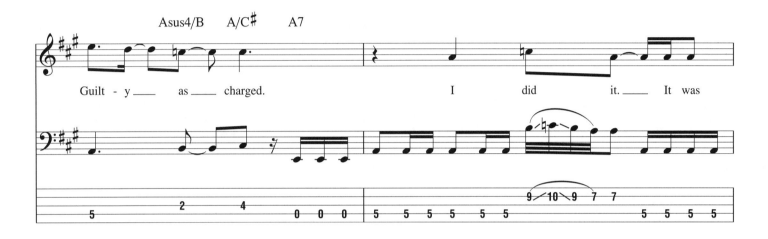

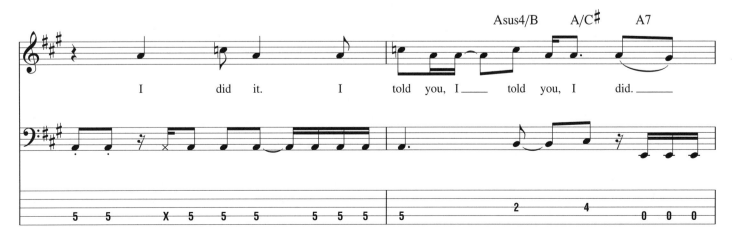

I did-n't know it felt__ so right__ in-side,__ I__ did-n't know at all.

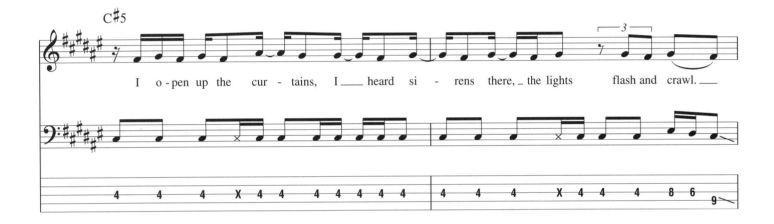

I o-pen up the cur - tains, I__ heard si - rens there,__ the lights flash and crawl.__

But I did it jus - tice. Well,__ I did it for us all__ you know.__

This Love

Words and Music by Adam Levine and Jesse Carmichael

5-stg. bass:
(low to high) B-E-A-D-G

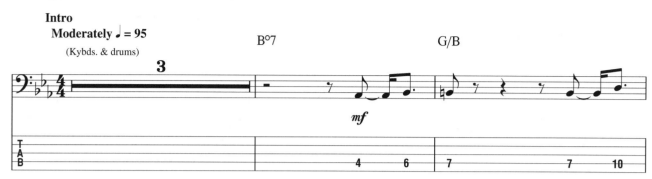

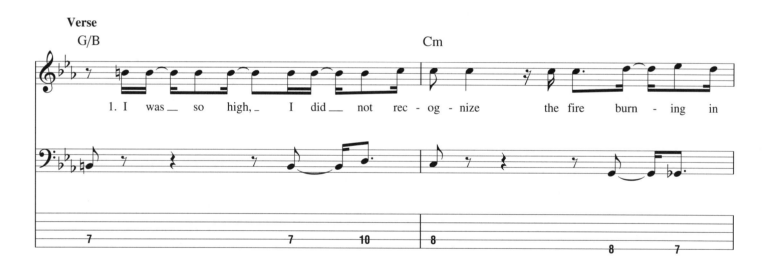

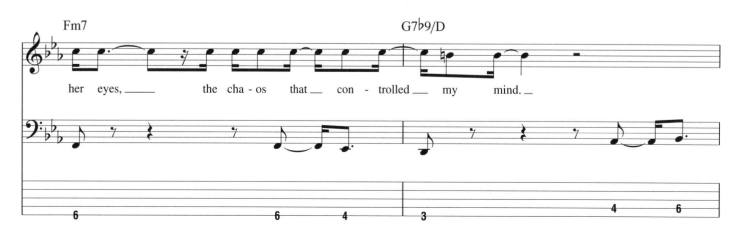

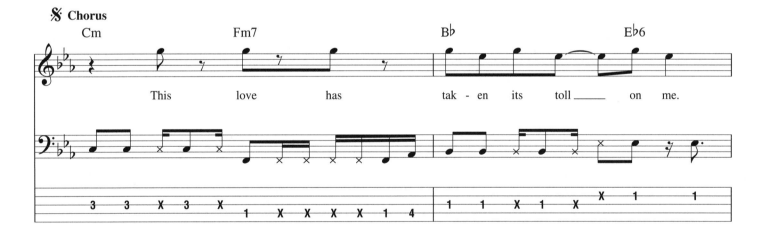

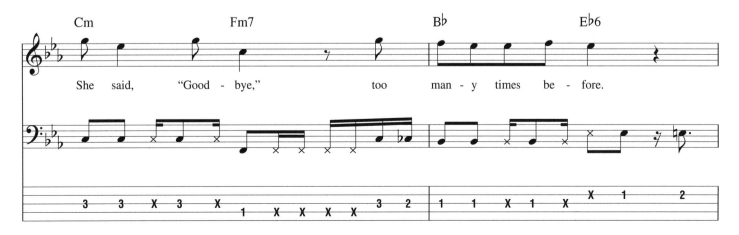

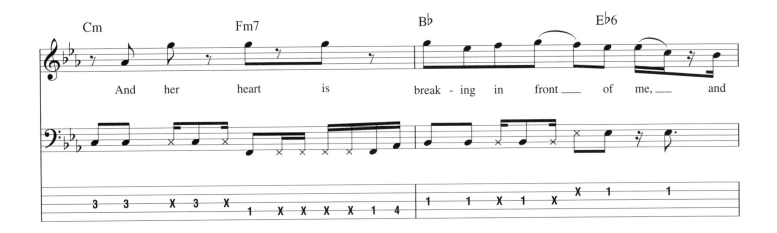

Cm   Fm7   Bb   Eb6

And her heart is break - ing in front of me, and

Cm   F   Fm7/Ab   G

I have no choice 'cause I won't say "Good - bye," an - y - more.

To Coda ⊕

Interlude

G/B   Cm   Fm7

Whoa, whoa, whoa,

Verse

G7/D   G/B

whoa. 2. I tried my best to feed her ap -

D.S. al Coda

⊕ **Coda**

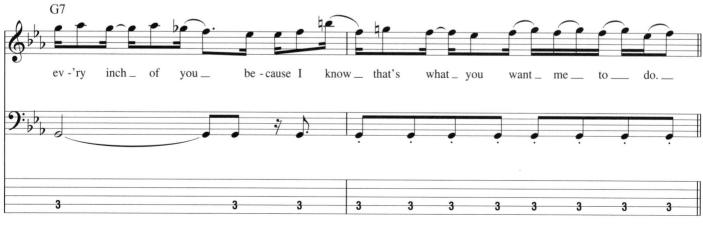

Outro-Chorus

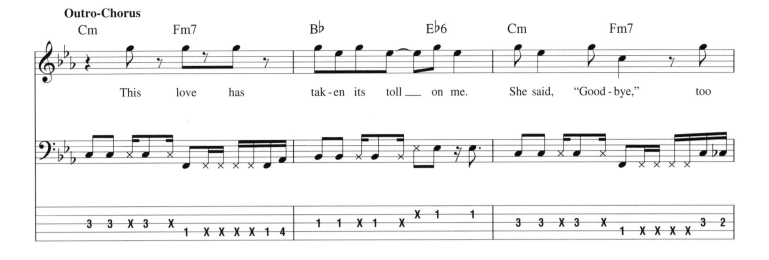

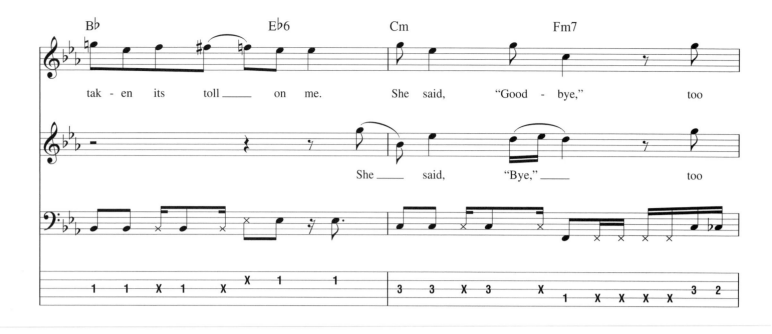

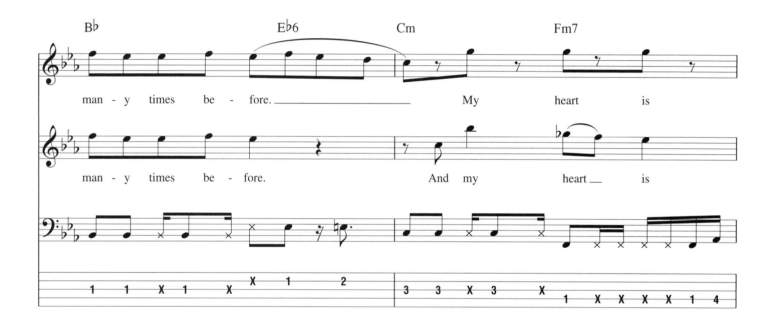

It's My Life

Words and Music by Mark Hollis and Tim Friese-Greene

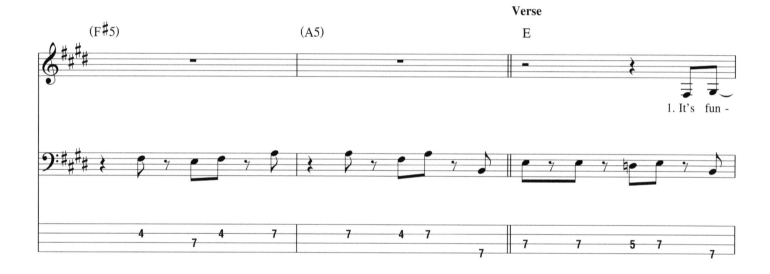

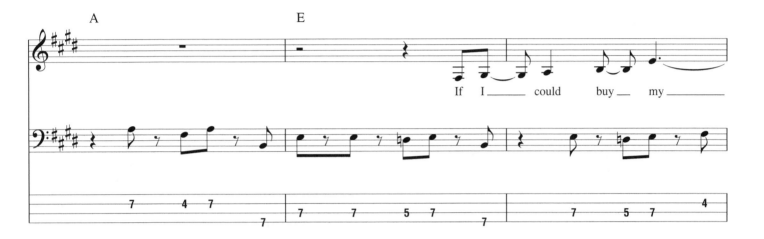

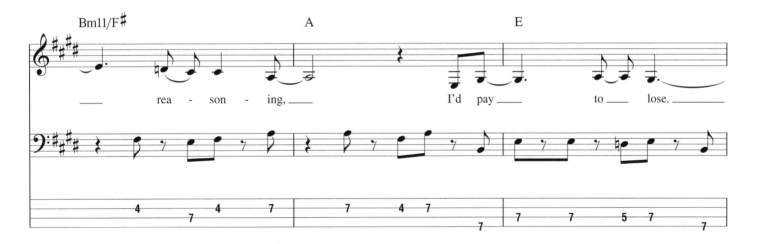

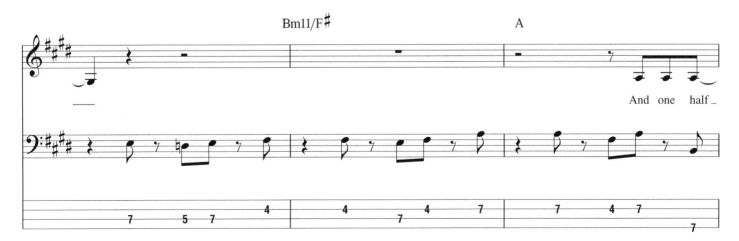

Coda 1

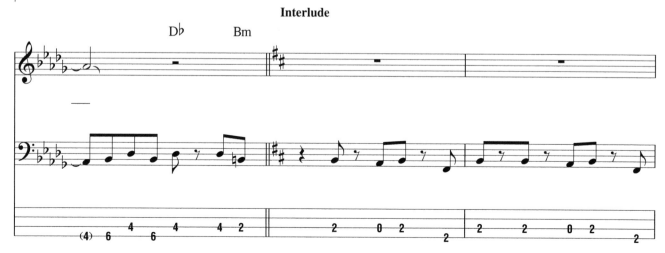

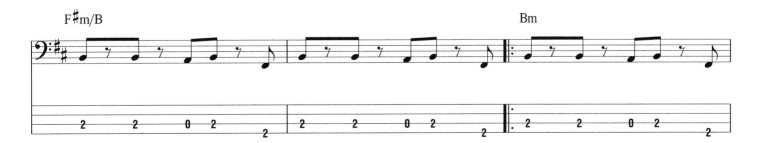

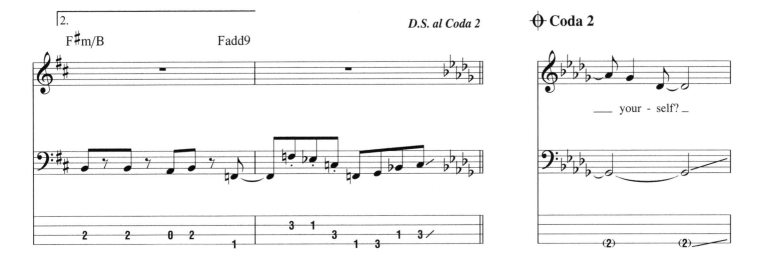

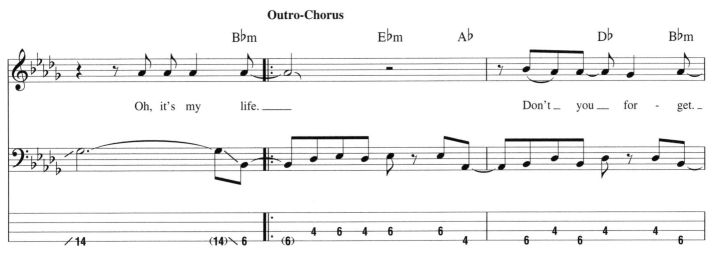

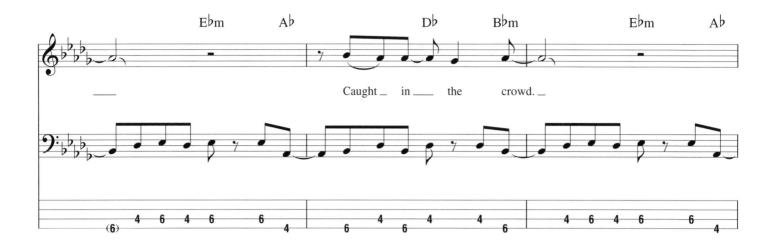

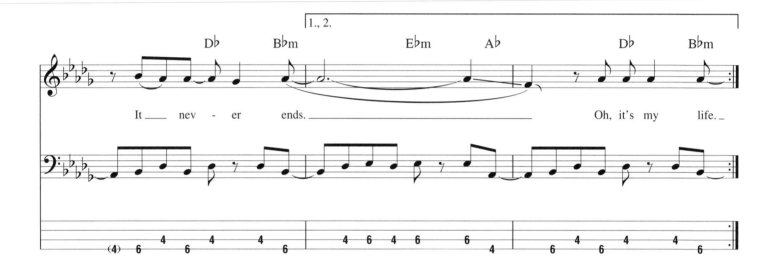

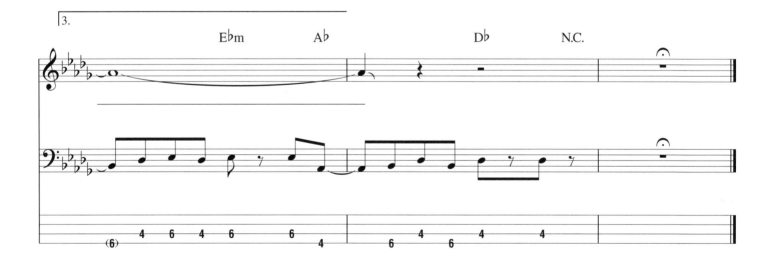

Additional Lyrics

Pre-Chorus 2. Oh, I'd tell myself,
What good do you do,
Convince myself.

HAL·LEONARD BASS PLAY·ALONG

The Bass Play-Along Series will help you play your favorite songs quickly and easily! Just follow the tab, listen to the CD to hear how the bass should sound, and then play along using the separate backing tracks. The melody and lyrics are also included in the book in case you want to sing, or to simply help you follow along. The CD is enhanced so you can use your computer to adjust the recording to any tempo without changing pitch!

1. Rock
Another One Bites the Dust • Badge • Brown Eyed Girl • Come Together • The Joker • Low Rider • Money • Sweet Emotion.
00699674 Book/CD Pack......................................$12.95

2. R&B
Get Ready • I Can't Help Myself (Sugar Pie, Honey Bunch) • I Got You (I Feel Good) • I Heard It Through the Grapevine • I Want You Back • In the Midnight Hour • My Girl • You Can't Hurry Love.
00699675 Book/CD Pack......................................$12.95

3. Pop/Rock
Crazy Little Thing Called Love • Crocodile Rock • Maneater • My Life • No Reply at All • Peg • Message in a Bottle • Suffragette City.
00699677 Book/CD Pack......................................$12.95

4. '90s Rock
All I Wanna Do • Fly Away • Give It Away • Hard to Handle • Jeremy • Know Your Enemy • Spiderwebs • You Oughta Know.
00699679 Book/CD Pack......................................$12.95

5. Funk
Brick House • Cissy Strut • Get Off • Get Up (I Feel Like Being) a Sex Machine • Higher Ground • Le Freak • Pick up the Pieces • Super Freak.
00699680 Book/CD Pack......................................$12.95

6. Classic Rock
Free Ride • Funk #49 • Gimme Three Steps • Green-Eyed Lady • Radar Love • Werewolves of London • White Room • Won't Get Fooled Again.
00699678 Book/CD Pack......................................$12.95

7. Hard Rock
Crazy Train • Detroit Rock City • Iron Man • Livin' on a Prayer • Living After Midnight • Peace Sells • Smoke on the Water • The Trooper.
00699676 Book/CD Pack......................................$14.95

8. Punk Rock
Brain Stew • Buddy Holly • Dirty Little Secret • Fat Lip • Flavor of the Weak • Gotta Get Away • Lifestyles of the Rich and Famous • Man Overboard.
00699813 Book/CD Pack......................................$12.95

9. Blues
All Your Love (I Miss Loving) • Born Under a Bad Sign • I'm Tore Down • I'm Your Hoochie Coochie Man • Killing Floor • Pride and Joy • Sweet Home Chicago • The Thrill Is Gone.
00699817 Book/CD Pack $12.95

10. Jimi Hendrix Smash Hits
All Along the Watchtower • Can You See Me? • Crosstown Traffic • Fire • Foxey Lady • Hey Joe • Manic Depression • Purple Haze • Red House • Remember • Stone Free • The Wind Cries Mary.
00699815 Book/CD Pack $16.95

11. Country
Achy Breaky Heart (Don't Tell My Heart) • All My Ex's Live in Texas • Boot Scootin' Boogie • Chattahoochee • Guitars, Cadillacs • I Like It, I Love It • Should've Been a Cowboy • T-R-O-U-B-L-E.
00699818 Book/CD Pack $12.95

13. Lennon & McCartney
All My Loving • Back in the U.S.S.R. • Day Tripper • Eight Days a Week • Get Back • I Saw Her Standing There • Nowhere Man • Paperback Writer.
00699816 Book/CD Pack $14.99

14. Modern Rock
Aerials • Duality • Here to Stay • I Stand Alone • Judith • Nice to Know You • Nookie • One Step Closer.
00699821 Book/CD Pack......................................$14.99

16. '80s Metal
Big City Nights • (Bang Your Head) Metal Health • Rock Me • Rock of Ages • Shot in the Dark • Talk Dirty to Me • We're Not Gonna Take It • Yankee Rose.
00699825 Book/CD Pack......................................$16.99

17. Pop Metal
Beautiful Girls • Breaking the Chains • Cult of Personality • Get the Funk Out • Heaven's on Fire • Livin' on a Prayer • No More Tears • Up All Night.
00699826 Book/CD Pack......................................$14.99

19. Steely Dan
Deacon Blues • Do It Again • FM • Hey Nineteen • Josie • Peg • Reeling in the Years • Rikki Don't Lose That Number.
00700203 Book/CD Pack......................................$16.99

21. Rock Band – Modern Rock
Are You Gonna Be My Girl • Black Hole Sun • Creep • Dani California • In Bloom • Learn to Fly • Say It Ain't So • When You Were Young.
00700705 Book/CD Pack $14.95

22. Rock Band – Classic Rock
Ballroom Blitz • Detroit Rock City • Don't Fear the Reaper • Gimme Shelter • Highway Star • Mississippi Queen • Suffragette City • Train Kept A-Rollin'.
00700706 Book/CD Pack $14.95

23. Pink Floyd – Dark Side of The Moon
Any Colour You Like • Brain Damage • Breathe • Eclipse • Money • Time • Us and Them.
00700847 Book/CD Pack......................................$14.99

24. Weezer
Beverly Hills • Buddy Holly • Dope Nose • Hash Pipe • My Name Is Jonas • Pork and Beans • Say It Ain't So • Undone – The Sweater Song.
00700960 Book/CD Pack......................................$14.99

25. Nirvana
All Apologies • Come As You Are • Dumb • Heart Shaped Box • In Bloom • Lithium • Rape Me • Smells like Teen Spirit.
00701047 Book/CD Pack......................................$14.99

33. Christmas Hits
Blue Christmas • The Christmas Song (Chestnuts Roasting on an Open Fire) • Do You Hear What I Hear • Frosty the Snow Man • Here Comes Santa Claus (Right Down Santa Claus Lane) • Jingle-Bell Rock • Let It Snow! Let It Snow! Let It Snow! • Silver Bells.
00701197 Book/CD Pack......................................$12.99

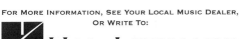

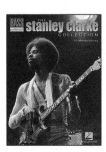
    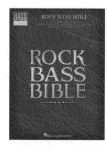 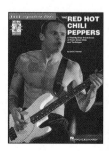